A Year in the Grief Valley:

365 Days of Love and Loss

John Pavlovitz

Parson's Porch Books

A Year in the Grief Valley: 365 Days of Love and Loss

ISBN: Softcover 978-1-951472-34-4

To order additional copies of this book, contact:

Parson's Porch Books 1-423-475-7308
www.parsonsporch.com

Parson's Porch Books is an imprint of Parson's Porch & Company (PP&C) in Cleveland, Tennessee. PP&C is an innovative non-profit organization which raises money by publishing books of noted authors, representing all genres. All donations from contributors and profits from publishing are shared with the poor.

A Year in the Grief Valley

FOREWORD

Even though my path takes me through the Grief Valley, I will walk without fear. Psalm 23 Paraphrase

Grief is a solitary road.

Even if we are fortunate enough to have people alongside us during the journey, (as I have been), no one can really travel all the way with us. Our pain and our path are as individual as the relationship we share with the person we've lost.

When my father died suddenly back in September of 2013, I began doing what I always do: I started writing. I did it to somehow make sense of my own grief, and to keep moving through the place I now call The Grief Valley.

These seven short chapters, (the first one written just three days after his passing) are some of the most personal things I've ever shared. They're also some of the writings I'm most proud of.

I've collected them here, in the hopes that they will be an encouragement and source of comfort for those experiencing loss of someone they love dearly, though I know each path will be a completely different one.

This work represents a real-time processing of my first year without my Dad. It's not a "how-to" book by any means, but maybe in my story, you'll find

5

something that you yourself can own; something to make your personal road through the Grief Valley a little more bearable.

Be encouraged. Keep walking.

HANDLE WITH CARE: MY WEEK AS A GRIEF ZOMBIE

September 17th, 2013

My dad died very suddenly, three days ago.

The first few seconds of that morning phone call, will be burned into my memory for the rest of my life; the one where I heard my youngest brother's voice quivering, as he told me that my father had passed away in his sleep while on a cruise with my mom on his 70th birthday. The words sent me immediately to my knees on the front lawn, and sometimes I feel like I'm still there, at least a good part of my heart is.

Since then, I've been what I would call a Grief Zombie; walking around in an odd, contradictory haze of searing pain and complete numbness, which both like to take rapid turns overpowering me. It's as-if you're being sucker punched by sadness one second, and bear-hugged by gratitude the next.

But all the while since that life-altering phone call, (as those who have experienced the loss of someone they love, know), I've had to continue to do stuff; take the kids to school, buy bananas, go to the gym; partly because things still need to get done, and partly because these mundane, ordinary tasks, help keep you from completely losing it in the face of the pure insanity of your reality.

Over the last three days, as I've navigated parking lots, waited in restaurant lines, and sat on park benches, I've done so, pushing back tears, fighting to stay upright, and in general; being just seconds from a total, blubbering, room-clearing freak out.

I've felt like I've wanted to wear a sign that says: I JUST LOST MY DAD. PLEASE GO EASY. I mean, other than my embarrassingly bloodshot eyes, and the occasional puberty-recalling break in my voice, it's not like anyone would know what's happening inside me or around me.

And while I don't want to physically wear my actual circumstances on my chest, I know that if I did, it would probably cause people around me to give me space, or speak softer, or move more carefully, and it would probably make the impossible, almost bearable.

But even as I've wished that people could see the personal Hell that I'm going through, I'm aware of the acute blindness that I myself usually live with, and the tremendous ego that exists in the request itself.

Why am I so special? Why is my pain any more pressing than anyone else's? Why do I assume that everybody but me is alright? Why do I expect everyone around me to be any sturdier than I feel right now?

This week, I've been reminded that I am surrounded by Grief Zombies all the time. Maybe they aren't mourning the sudden, tragic passing of a parent; but wounded, broken, pain-ravaged people are everywhere, everyday, stumbling around, and yet most of them time, I'm fairly oblivious to them:

Parents whose children are terminally ill.

Couples in the middle of divorce.

Kids being bullied at school.

Teenagers who want to end their lives.

Spouses whose partners are deployed in combat.

Families with no idea how to keep the lights on. Young moms with little help, little sleep, and less sympathy.

Yet none of them wear the signs. None of them have labels. None of them come with written warnings reading: FRAGILE: HANDLE WITH CARE.

And since they don't, it's up to you and me to look more closely and more deeply at everyone around us; at work, or at the gas station, or in the produce section, and never assume they aren't all just hanging by a thread.

We need to remind ourselves just how hard the stories around us might be, and to approach each person, as a delicate, breakable, invaluable treasure, and to go easy.

As you walk, drive and click around this week, people won't be wearing signs, but if you look with the right eyes, you'll see the signs.

Life is fragile... Hold it carefully.   People

are fragile... Handle them gently.

You are fragile... Take it easy.

Valley Reflections

1. The only right way to grieve; is the way that you are grieving right now. There's no guide or rules here in the Valley. Your loss, and the working through of that loss will be as unique as the relationship you had with your loved one. Don't try to steer this thing.

2. Pain is a really good teacher. How is your own grief helping you see and be aware of the suffering around you? As difficult as these days are for you, how can they help you view others with a compassion that you might never otherwise have had?

3. Right now, the ordinary, mundane tasks may seem trivial in the light of your loss, but do them. More than just keeping you busy, they will help you stay connected to Life, even as you grieve your experience with Death. The ordinary things are more important than you think.

FINDING MY KRYPTONITE

October 6th, 2013

These are weird days in Metropolis.

Ever since my father passed away suddenly three weeks ago, there isn't much about life that isn't profoundly different; from the way the nighttime feels, to the tightening in my stomach whenever the phone rings, to the way I see my children, to the way I imagine the rest of my life.

I think differently, I sense time differently, and I look at the future differently as well.

But more than anything, the grief I've experienced since the loss of my dad, has led me to a clear and startling admission: I'm not a superhero.

For the past 17 years as a pastor, I've made a living saving people; of dramatically flying into the burning rubble of other's lives and coming out without a scratch, carrying the grateful mortals I've rescued... or so I thought.

OK, maybe I haven't pictured myself in quite those grandiose terms, but I've certainly seen myself as a problem solver, a fixer, a leader; someone to be counted on.

I've prided myself on being professional, and excellent, and dependable, and like many in ministry, I've been the person others come to for help. If there've been bullets to outrun, trains to overpower, or tall buildings to leap over, I've been your man; or rather, your Super-man.

Then I ran into Kryptonite.

Ever since I learned of my father's death, I've felt decidedly human; and been brought, both figuratively and literally, to my knees. I've found myself unable to focus, or stay engaged, or control my emotions... (You know, just like an actual person).

For the first time, maybe ever, I've had to admit to others (and to myself), that I need the saving. And for the first time, I've taken the costume and the cape off, and stopped being so damn super.

It's a pretty tough thing for any would-be hero to face weakness; to acknowledge when they're reached the end of their strength; when they are broken, defeated, failing.

I think many of you understand that. I think you've been wearing the costume for a while yourself, too.

OK, so maybe you're not an overachieving pastor. Maybe you're a superstar at work, or a perfectionist parent, or a superhuman spouse, or a school sports star, or an academic sensation.

Maybe you've gained some attention, or recognition, or reputation by being great at something, and ever since, you've become, on some level, in your own situation; a superhero.

13

Maybe you just find your identity and your worth through your pursuit of perfection.

Lots of us live with inflated perceptions of ourselves; straddled with unrealistic expectations and unreasonable goals, either from outside or from within, we strive and strain to keep it all together; to earn the accolades, to get the grade, to look the part, to get the prize, and to do everything short of saving the world.

And setting down the weight of the planet isn't easy, once you're convinced that you're supposed to be carrying it; that it's your job to keep it all up and spinning.

In fact, if you fancy yourself a superhero, most people will be content to hand you a costume, point you to a phone booth, and cheer you on from the street below.

If you've stumbled upon this writing, and you're exhausted from being superhuman, whether at home or school, or in your marriage, or at your job, please hear me: You can take off the costume.

We all have our Kryptonite, and we all reach the capacity of our power. We all find ourselves bruised and bloodied and beaten-up by this life, and yet the great news, is that even then, we can endure.

Only we don't do it on our strength, or with our ability or charisma or intellect.

Sometimes we move forward, only as we are carried on the shoulders of others. I am learning this these days.

The past three weeks have been incredibly painful, but so freeing too. It's a pretty powerful thing, to admit when you are powerless.

Maybe, like me, you'll need to hit some traumatic turn in your road to realize all this, but I'm hoping not.

Perhaps you'll see these words, as permission to be imperfect; to not have it all together, to fail and fall and cry, and to be carried for a while.

I'm retiring from the superhero business, and I'm asking you to join me.

Ditch the spandex, friend.

Welcome to humanity.

Valley Reflections

1. You're probably feeling pretty broken and weak right now, to say the least. If you're used to going through life as a superhero, that can be a rude awakening. Grief has a way of equalizing us; forcing us all to our knees. Let yourself be defeated right now. Give yourself permission to fall. Be a mortal for a while.

2. Tears are a tribute. That's a phrase that's been with me since the first few days of my journey through The Grief Valley. Regardless of whether or not you were an emotional person prior to this experience, you may be now. One of the greatest pieces of wisdom I heard about Grief is that it is the tax on loving people. Your tears are a payment.

3. Where are you feeling pressure right now to "get over it"; to be strong or to keep a stiff upper-lip in the face of your Grief? It may be from others, or you may be bringing this upon yourself. Either way, realize that this is unhelpful advice. Your recovery has no deadline. In fact, this will be something you're never finished with, so don't rush to be through with whatever you're feeling right now.

WHEN "A BETTER PLACE" AIN'T BETTER

October 23rd, 2013

Words are wild, unpredictable things.

Often, ones delivered in love and designed to heal can wound terribly, especially when attempting to help someone dealing with death.

In trying to help you weather the loss of a loved one, kindhearted, well-meaning people will often tell you that those you mourn over, have "gone to a better place".

Though said earnestly, and always in love, this is almost never very helpful or comforting, as grief is really about the personal sense of loss one feels in the here and now.

For survivors, this is largely about how stinkin' lousy this place currently is.

When you're dealing with crippling pain, and with the unfathomable newly-made hole in your life; when you're just trying to piece together in your mind, a patchwork of coherent thoughts to make the present bearable, the phrase "a better place", often adds insult to horrific injury.

Yes, you want goodness for your loved one, and you think about all that they cannot and will not experience here, and yes, the thought of them in Heaven, free from pain and worry is a small help;

17

but you're also pretty darn selfish about the whole thing, too.

To the grieving mind, the pushback to this idea comes easy, if we think about it:

Heaven was already a better place before all of this happened, but this loss, and the void it has created for the heart in the Valley, has now made this place, (the place where those left behind have to stay and live), a much, much worse place.

And in this sadly ironic way, the seemingly innocent words that you hope will bring comfort, can actually amplify the loss for a survivor; magnifying the great chasm between them, and the one they no longer have.

"Heaven gained an angel", is another similar well-meaning, but greatly flawed attempt at consolation. Again, it's a beautiful image and a seemingly sweet idea, but for those carrying on here in the Valley, it's mixed with the horrible reality that we, living where angels are already in very short supply as it is, have had yet another casualty.

Please don't hear this as a slight to you, if you've ever spoken these words to someone you love; even to me.

They're ones that I've offered as well at one time or another, and in those moments, I too was lovingly, desperately grasping for something that could help carry someone else as they wept. I know well, that those words are simply all you can think to do to reach into a loved one's pain and try and pull them out.

The only problem is, the Grief valley is a place out where words can't come and where they don't help.

It's just another reminder and a lesson for the heart, that when facing the irrevocable, irreplaceable loss of someone you held dear, even the most loving words fail.

In the end, the only thing we can offer someone we care for, that can provide the kind of comfort that we all wish words will, are prayers and presence.

There's something about simply being with someone; about sitting with them in a pain that you refrain from speaking into that allows stuff much bigger and far greater than words to be exchanged. And in reality, to the one grieving, that presence is what they'll remember.

Only in those sacred moments of silent presence, can the power of that "better place", really be felt anyway. So come as far in as you can to walk with alongside those you love, but leave your words outside.

A lesson I'm learning in the Valley.

Valley Reflections

1. Have you had damaging or unhelpful words spoken to you by people regarding your Grief? Resist the tendency to get angry or resent those delivering them. They are almost always trying to do the impossible; to fix this with words. Even as you are suffering, have gratitude for the efforts of those who misstep.

2. Can you think of words that can describe your Grief right now? If you had to put it into words for others to understand, what would you say?

3. Where do you find comfort right now? What things, people, activities bring you peace and rest? What places are most difficult? Pay attention to the ways the rhythms of life are part of your grieving.

4. We often give people eulogies after their gone, but have difficulty honoring people while they're here. Consider giving someone you love a "living eulogy" today, by saying, typing, texting, or writing words that celebrate them.

IN THE WIDTH OF A BREATH

April 5th, 2014

It's now been six months since my father passed away suddenly, while on a cruise with my Mom and brother.

I'd like to say that things have gotten easier since then, that the pain isn't still crippling at times, that I've come to terms with the fact that I won't get to share life with him anymore; but that would be a lie.

I'd like to say that I've made peace with the pain, but I'm not sure you ever really do that.

What's so unbelievable at times, is the ways in which grief waves hit you.

Sadness often springs its cruel surprise party; jumping out of bushes, or from behind grocery store aisles, or from inside the hall closet. The simple, ordinary, sometimes completely unrelated stuff that derails and devastates you is staggering; smells, sounds, food, sitcoms, songs, breezes, temperature.

Lately, one of the things that's been my constant companion in the Grief Valley, is the idea of thinness; of the stark, brutal, incomprehensibly small space between living, and leaving.

My father died in his sleep on the ship, following a birthday dinner filled with food and laughter, and with the usual excitement and promise of the first day at sea.

As far as any of us can tell, he experienced no pain, no trauma, and no anguish.

He simply went to sleep, and stayed asleep.

As he closed his eyes, it probably never occurred to him that these were his last hours here; no soul-searching, no fond looking back, no final words, no dramatic speeches.

I want to feel relief, but what I really feel is cheated.

I'll never forget one of the first things my mother said when I spoke to her on the phone from the ship: "He had a beautiful death."

It was, in its gentleness and swiftness indeed beautiful, but here a half-a-year removed, it's that same silent suddenness that's really messing with me.

I picture his face in that moment lying there in bed; as he quietly passed from this life into what is beyond it; no fanfare or drama or bombast. He just breathed... and then he didn't.

His heart was beating, and then it ceased to.

And in that most infinitesimal of spaces, my father's 70-year life was over, and so many others were irrevocably, completely altered.

In the width of one breath, everything changed for me. In the space that small, the Grief Valley opened-up and sucked me in.

I've heard and spoken all the words about how quickly life moves and about how fragile it is, and those words have never been truer than they have these past six months.

However, what's both infuriating and frightening, (and yet somehow beautifully sweet), is just how thin it all is.

Honestly, I'm not sure what to do with this revelation as I type this; other than feel like I'm reading aloud some saccharine-soaked greeting card platitudes about loving the people around you while they're here, and about living your life to the fullest, and about not sweating the small stuff; but that's horribly underselling the gravity of it all.

Besides, there are some lessons that can only really be learned when looking back, and sadly the Grief Valley is something you simply can't walk through until you're in it.

My faith tells me that on a September night, in a cruise ship bed, in that thinnest of expanses, my father went from conscious, to much-more-than conscious; that without ever waking-up, he suddenly received the answers to the questions that everyone on this side of the thinness wonders about.

And yet some days I confess as I ponder all of it, that my faith too becomes the thinness. It sometimes stretches to a paper-width place, as hope and grief pull from opposite ends, and where I strain to look for the light breaking through.

And it's in that place, where somehow, God is closest.

One breath here, the next breath, hereafter.

That, is life and death; the great, glorious thinness.

Valley Reflections

1. How is your time in the Grief Valley changing or affirming your ideas about Heaven and Hell; about the afterlife; about God? What, if anything is happening in your belief system right now? Are you discovering faith, or increasing it, doubting it, or abandoning it?

2) If you can come up with anything, what are the blessings you've experienced during your Grief? What lessons have you learned or what knowledge have you received that you would have never received otherwise?

3) Knowing how thin life is, pay attention to the places and the people who give yours meaning. Celebrate, enjoy, and give thanks for them. Do something today that is life-affirming.

ATTRITION AND AMPUTATION: LOSING AND LIMPING IN THE GRIEF VALLEY

April 29th, 2014

My dad died nearly 8 months ago, and some stuff is finally starting to settle.

There are realities that hit you little by little as you grieve; brutal truths that you've probably really known for a lot longer, but that you couldn't quite wrap your brain around enough to claim as your own.

Maybe it's your mind's way of protecting itself from bearing too much sadness, too much trauma at one time.

One of the things that's become clear in recent weeks, is the simple reality that my life will not get better.

That's not to say that I won't feel better, or that the sadness won't eventually recede somewhat, or that there won't be really, really good moments. (I've experienced all of this in the months following my Dad's passing).

I know in the future, that I'll laugh bombastically, and eat decadent meals, and be moved by music, and I'll travel, and dance, and create, and feel moments of true joy and contentment.

When I say that I know that life won't get better though, it's admitting the sobering truth, that despite all of these incredible, gratitude-inducing, live-giving things that will surely come; my life will simply never be as good as it was when my father was in this world.

It will never be better, than it was before he left.

It couldn't be.

No matter who or what I add to my journey, or what victories or successes they bring, they will never replace the part that's gone; the part uniquely shaped like him.

It would be an insult to my father and to his unimaginable impact in my life, to expect otherwise.

I guess that's why the word loss, while seemingly incomplete, says it all pretty darn well as you grieve.

When you do lose someone close to you, you learn to make peace with attrition; with the cruel, horrible subtraction that death delivers. You realize that there was a time, (now in the past), when your family was whole, and that no matter what the future brings, it will now always remain less-than.

I imagine it's not unlike the way a new amputee feels, as they move though life without a leg.

They adapt, they learn to cope and relearn to navigate daily tasks; they find creative, amazing ways to do everything that they did before, but it's always a reaction to damage.

It's always an attempt to respond to invasive intrusion; to get as close as they can to wholeness, to completeness, and yet there's just no way to get it all back.

You live, but you live with a limp.

That's what grieving is. That's what the attrition causes.   You do move forward, but it's only because it's the only direction you have left, if you want to keep living.

You take every painful, awkward, desperate step it takes to keep walking, and you try to go as far as you can, with what you've lost.

This probably comes across as pretty depressing stuff, but for me, it's a gift; helping me clearly see and appreciate the present.

Most likely, this won't be the last time I'll grieve someone I love, and when that unwanted day and time does come, I'll look back and remember these days and these times, as ones when I was a little closer to whole.

For everyone reading this in The Grief Valley, struggling to take the next excruciating step; be encouraged.

Yes, you've lost something irreplaceable, but you haven't lost it all.

There's still a good, beautiful, blessing-filled path for you to walk.

So walk on, even if it is with a limp.

Valley Reflections

1. What do you miss the most about the loved one you've lost? What are the things you can't get back or do again that are the most painful right now? Make a list, as short or as long as you feel like.

2. What things and people still give you joy; music, food, laughter, nature, relationships. Today, try not to grieve what is no longer, but to celebrate what life is. Make some time today to give thanks for the good stuff in your now.

3. That hole you feel that's been created by the absence of the one you've lost? Realize that you occupy that kind of space for others. Your life is powerful and meaningful to so many. As a way to affirm that, reach out to someone who loves you today; someone who would miss your presence if you were gone, and simply spend some time with them.

BLOOD BREAKS THROUGH THE SKIN

July 29th, 2014

Blood is fascinating.

It's so full of life, so critical to every breath and step; a powerful, perpetual flood, flowing just there beneath the surface of our skin. It's a force that we're largely quite oblivious to as well, even as it's part of us, even as it sustains us.

In fact, we don't think much about our blood until something breaks the flesh, and we realize just how close we are to it all. Sometimes it takes so little to bring it rushing to the surface, and then the challenge is to stop it before it does too much damage.

Grief is this way.

It's hidden, just there beneath the visible stuff of life.

Some days, we who've lost someone we love are quite unaware it's still there at all.

We forget the river raging underneath.

Sometimes, for stretches of hours or even days or weeks, we move and plan and laugh, and play with our kids, and go to restaurants, and mow the lawn, and fold laundry, and Tweet our dessert photos, and everything feels normal, and then it happens; a little pin prick, and a wound opens.

The stuff that breaks the surface and triggers the flood of sadness and memory in the wake of loss, is confoundingly random, often so innocuous that it seems ridiculous; that is, until the abrasion.

The most mundane, trivial things can derail you in The Grief Valley; much like that split-second slip of your finger opening a can, or the sudden misstep walking in the garden that can cut the skin, turning an ordinary moment into Triage duty.

Here, ten months after my father's passing, I find (among a million other places), that solitary trips to a local grocery store do this for me. For no reason that makes any real sense, I often find myself pushing back tears in the breakfast cereal aisle or the produce section. (Awkward for the clerks and customers, I'm sure).

And as silly as is sounds, that's the place where I grieve fully; the place where I so often bleed and bandage, and where I again face the rushing, hidden flood.

There is no rhyme or reason to things that reopen the wounds for any of us. There is no sense to Grief. It simply comes when it chooses, and it makes you bleed.

Over time, you learn to accept that the stuff beneath the surface just isn't going away... ever. You may develop thicker skin, or you may be less apt to break as often as before, but the flood is still there below; of sweet memories, and wasted words, and missed opportunities, and lost tomorrows.

I think walking through this Valley for the past 10 months has helped me realize just how much is happening right below the surface for all of us.

I don't just see people now. I try to see into them.

I know that there is more than they show, and more than their exposed surface skin reveals. I know that at any moment, they may be bleeding and they may need bandaging.

Look around for those in your path who may be walking wounded, and who simply aren't showing it.

See deeper than skin.

If you're navigating your own loss these days; be aware of the river of grief beneath your own flesh, and make peace with the fact that it won't stay hidden forever.

Valley Reflections

1. When's the last time you were surprised by Grief, even the most innocuous and unrelated circumstances? What's a place or time when you seem to grieve fully?

2. Looking back at the way you reacted to other's loss in the past, did you ever fail to appreciate the depth of pain they were in? How has your own journey through The Grief Valley changed your understanding of people facing the death of someone they love?

3. Can you think of someone in your life right who is going through Grief right now? Today, think about reaching-out to them. In your woundedness, you still have a tremendous capacity; maybe more than ever, to heal.

A YEAR TO LIFE: MY FIRST 365 DAYS IN THE GRIEF VALLEY

September 13th, 2014

It's the year anniversary of Day 1 in the Grief Valley.

I really thought today would feel different.

A year ago today, my father spent his 70th birthday departing on a West Coast cruise with my mother and other members of our family. He posed for the requisite sail-away photos, had a celebratory first night dinner, took a relaxing walk around the ship, went to bed... and never woke-up.

In many ways I feel like I'm still sleeping too; still expecting to wake-up from all of this.

Most people speak about how difficult the nights are after you lose someone you love, but for me it's the mornings that have been the cruelest. So many dawns with grief, you feel it fresh when you open your eyes and look round and you realize; "Crap, this actually happened".

And it's like that very first horrible day all over again.

365 days in the Grief Valley, and I was hoping for some grand revelation today, some brilliant moment of clarity; a dramatic turning point upon which I could pivot and sprint toward some sort of emotional resolution.

I desperately prayed that I could pass along a sacred nugget of truth today that might help you too; you who are in the Valley with me.

I don't think that's coming.

Thankfully, as so often has been the story of my life; music has spoken the cries of my heart, tapping into the deep recesses of pain where words are hard to come by, and given me words.

Like a letter from an old friend, this was in my music library this week: I know there is no end to grief, that's how I know there is no end to love. - Bono, California

That's pretty much the deal.

This really is the story of The Grief Valley; once you enter it, you never really ever leave again. And the most ironic thing, is that you don't want to either.

To leave the Valley, would mean to leave behind love, because love for another is the source of the loss, and it's that loss that fuels the grieving.

And since you can't ever walk away from that love for the one you've lost; you take it with you, and you make peace with the reality that your life is now and forever a Valley life.

Yes, there are days when you get to a precious bit of clearing and you feel the sun more fully; days when you laugh and eat great food, and dance, and

36

dream; days when you almost feel like you've stepped through it all for good.

But it's never very long until you look-up and you realize that the mountains aren't gone; your eyes have just learned to adjust to their shadows.

Everything is saturated with memory, and so everything is what reminds you of the love and the loss.

I understand now that the pain of the absence of my dad isn't going anywhere. It couldn't, so long as his absence replaces his presence. That brutal separation will be here, no matter how much time passes.

Because my love for my father will remain until my last breath here, so will the pain of his passing; no end to Love, no end to Grief.

I've come to accept that I'll share my days with both of them, so we better all just get comfy.

Tears are a tribute.

That phrase has been with me since my first days in the Valley, and I'm still honoring my dad today, twelve months later. I don't fight them anymore, those tears. I welcome them. I cherish them. I celebrate them.

For me, they are conversation, and communion, and restoration, and resurrection.

Those tears are proof that Love and Grief persevere and they need to; because both remind us of the delicate sweetness of this life and those we live it with.

So in many ways, Day 365 is just another day in the lifetime sentence that Death hands you: One year to life in the Grief Valley.

Love.

Grieve.

Love.

Grieve.

Repeat.

This is what we do in the Grief Valley. Keep walking.

Valley Reflections

1. Grief never ends, at least while we're here. Wherever you are in your journey, realize that it isn't a matter of finishing something. Think or write about where you are today, and see it as a good place to be; as another step.

2. What lessons have you already learned in the Grief Valley? If you were to tell your story to others, what would your words of wisdom be? Write them down and consider and consider sharing them in some way.

3. Tears are a tribute, and so is the life you live now. Let today be a memorial service to the person you've lost, and a worship service if you are a person of faith.